EARLY ENTRANCE TO COLLEGE AS AN OPTION FOR HIGHLY GIFTED ADOLESCENTS

Alexander R. Pagnani

Cheryll M. Adams, Series Editor

ISBN: 978-0-9960866-7-7

National Association for Gifted Children
1331 H Street, NW, Suite 1001
Washington, DC 20005
202-785-4268
http://www.nagc.org

TABLE OF CONTENTS

INTRODUCTION

Sir Ken Robinson, an internationally renowned expert on education, creativity, and the arts, often asks his audiences a poignant question. "Why is it," he queries, "that we educate our children in batches based on age groups? Why is there this assumption that the most important thing children have in common is how old they are?"[1] The question, of course, is meant to be rhetorical, yet it certainly exposes a fundamental assumption of mainstream educational thought that we otherwise would simply take for granted. Anyone with experience around children, whether as an educator or parent, surely knows how greatly one child can vary from another, regardless of whether we are talking about physical, cognitive, or emotional characteristics and maturity levels. One child may be far beyond his or her peers in terms of academic competency, while another child struggles mightily to keep up. Another child may be emotionally invested in passionately contributing to battling major world problems such as stopping global warming or saving endangered species, while most students in his or her classroom would rather talk about what reality television program they watched the night before. Children, in other words, differ. The resulting challenge for schools and educators, therefore, is to recognize that simple fact and deliver appropriately individualized education whenever reasonably possible.

While Robinson is correct to question why we automatically group students by age, the good news is that modern schools and educators have at their disposal a host of pedagogical strategies and practices meant to provide an appropriate educational experience to each child, specific to that child's individual status as learner. Differentiation and curricular modification, for example, can provide increased challenge to many gifted students within a heterogeneously grouped classroom environment. Gifted pullout programs and advanced, ability-grouped classes provide others with specially tailored activities and assignments, meant to support and foster their academic and social development. For most gifted students, modifications such as these suffice. Their talents are recognized, nurtured, and furthered without further adjustments to the environment. For a few exceptionally gifted students, however, these standard modifications prove insufficient for creating the sort of educational environment necessary for the child to thrive. These students are typically so cognitively advanced and out-of-step with the traditional curriculum for their age group that they require a more drastic change in order to be suitably engaged and challenged. What these students most need, in many cases, is "radical acceleration," better known as "grade skipping" or "early promotion" to the next level of schooling.

In many school districts, these students are not able to access these options. Radical acceleration, whether to a more advanced grade or even to an early entrance to a college or university, has, for reasons that will be discussed later, become associated with a wide assortment of academic and socio-emotional fears and concerns for the child's well-being. Well-meaning teachers, guidance counselors, parents, and administrators worry that the child will struggle with the more advanced curriculum, have difficulty making friends with the older students, and eventually come to feel that they were rushed through their childhood. Meanwhile, these exceptionally bright students are left to tread water, going through the motions each day of school, hoping that today might be the day when they learn something new, exciting, and relevant to their lives... or more sadly, that today might be the day when they won't get in trouble for reading the lengthy novel that they try to keep hidden underneath their classroom desks. What happens to these students, whose talents burn so brightly that even typical pedagogical alterations and gifted pullout programs fail to adequately address their needs? Well, most of them presumably emerge from K-12 schooling bored, but fine. They're likely to progress to college and do perfectly well. Some, however, become so bored that they begin to question whether school is truly for them. "If I'm not learning anything, why do I need to be here?" they ask themselves daily, as the frustration builds.

EARLY COLLEGE ENTRANCE AS A SERVICE OPTION

Some students have the option of radical acceleration, specifically in the form of early college entrance. Early college entrance was and is considered as a viable educational strategy, with the goal of matching student needs with an appropriately rigorous curriculum and a supportive intellectual environment. Collegiate early entrance, commonly defined as the full matriculation to college of a student at least one year prior to his or her former grade-level peers, without having earned a high school diploma beforehand, has been quietly undergoing a renaissance of sorts. Early entrance, whether through an established program or on an individual basis, was once commonplace throughout the United States but fell out of favor in the 1950s due to growing concerns over students' social and emotional preparedness. Since that time, research documenting the positive academic outcomes of acceleration has caused many to reconsider the practice, and in the last few decades, roughly 20 colleges and universities have established specialized programs for students opting to enter college at an early age. That said, the exact number of "early entrance programs" currently in operation is a difficult figure to pin down, as a great deal hinges on which criteria or elements a person uses to distinguish the colleges with "programs" from the 80+ percent of colleges and universities in the United States that simply allow early entrance on an individual basis. Most research publications typically recognize at least 12 residential programs and at least 7 distinct commuter programs.

Key Features of Early Entrance Programs

While the vast majority of American colleges and universities have always allowed atypically young students to apply and gain admittance if they can demonstrate academic and maturational readiness, formal early entrance programs differ in six critically key respects.

1. The programs typically offer a structured, sheltered environment for their students, often in the form of a separate program space or specialized dormitory facility with a residential staff trained to support the academic, social, and emotional development of their adolescent charges.

2. The programs include specific strategies to help students transition to the academic rigors of college, either by providing specialized courses for program students or by allowing access to the college's regular classes yet providing watchful guidance, advising, and tutoring opportunities until students have fully adapted.

3. The programs carefully cultivate a fun, yet supervised social environment providing students with opportunities to meet exceptionally bright peers from across the state or country – something that rarely happened in their previous school settings.

4. The programs generally provide various types of emotional support to students, helping them if needed to navigate those thorny adolescent issues of identity and self with trained, professional support personnel who understand the unique challenges of the atypically young college student.

5. A growing number of early entrance programs have negotiated the ability to match college schedules with their state's high school graduation requirements, meaning that students may be able to earn a high school diploma while taking a full slate of university-level courses.

6. The programs are meant to be a means, not an end, and their final defining characteristic is that they work to gradually acclimate the student to general college life, so that after a certain number of years in the program, the students will be ready to leave and complete the remainder of their college years just as any other student would, in regular dorms, with regular classes, and regular extracurricular and social opportunities. For some of the early entrant population, this transition is an easy one as they stay at the institution where they began their program, and they are already familiar with the campus, classes, professors, and recreational activities. For others, the transition may be a little more challenging, as these students are those who elect to transfer to another institution for the remainder of their college years – commonly to a higher profile university or even an Ivy League school.

Recognizing the growing phenomenon of early college entrance, and the role this option can play in the healthy intellectual and social development of highly able students, there are four key topics concerning early entrance and the students who elect to participate. We will examine the historical context of early entrance to college, asking whether our forebears similarly educated children in the age-based "batches" that Sir Ken Robinson had described and examining the numerous sea changes in education that led to early entrance's highs and lows. Next, we will examine the prevalent attitudes of most parents and educators today regarding radical acceleration methods, such as grade skipping and early college entrance, identifying the most common fears that hold students back and ask whether educational research actually supports those assertions. We then take a closer look at the diversity of modern early entrance programs in the United States, exploring the wide range of programs that exist for students of different ages, interests, and future goals. Finally, we will explore some of the most commonly asked questions concerning the motivations and life experiences of students who choose to matriculate to college at an early age to help students, parents, and teachers understand whether early entrance might be an appropriate educational intervention for themselves, their child, or that one student in their class who seems to know every answer before they've even asked the question.

HISTORICAL TRENDS IN EARLY ENTRANCE

Similar to the trends in public opinion towards gifted education in general, popular support for collegiate early entrance has ebbed and flowed throughout American history. Discussing the topic would not have been necessary during the first century-and-a-half of our nation's history. Prior to the formation of compulsory public schooling, students in local schoolhouses were typically grouped and advanced based on content mastery rather than chronological age. As a result, it would have been seen as natural for a student to enter a higher grade or graduate upon demonstrating mastery of the curriculum, regardless of their chronological age. This notion held true for college in the nineteenth century as well, as even until the late 1800s college classrooms were commonly expected to contain a wide mix of student ages. Some educational historians, such as Joseph Kett[2], have claimed that distributions from age 12 to 20 were common for first-year university cohorts during this time and provoked no unease or concern.

While this system of promotion based on content mastery suited the purposes for which it was intended, four major factors began to converge in the early decades of the twentieth century, leading to a more age-based notion of school promotion. First, states began to pass laws mandating compulsory school attendance for all children. Second, educational expectations for all children began to rise, a trend that has continued steadily well into the modern era. Third, the rise of psychology led to the first major theories of child and cognitive development, many of which were based on age-driven ideas and stages, such as those of Jean Piaget. Fourth, increased immigration and mandatory schooling combined to create large increases in the number of children requiring educational services, thus leading cities, counties, and states to consider more big-picture, structurally organized approaches to education rather than relying on the traditional one-room schoolhouses of decades past. Even still, flexible notions of grade advancement based on content mastery were able to hold on for the first two decades of the twentieth century in some places, especially in major cities and on the west coast. In Lewis Terman's famous longitudinal study of gifted individuals the average participant actually graduated from high school at the age of 16, thereby demonstrating that "early entrance to college" was still the norm in his region of California as late as the 1920s.[3]

In addition to the four factors described above, another major cause of shifting attitudes nationwide against early entrance derived from the popular press's frenzy over the unfortunate case of William James Sidis.[4] Sidis, a remarkably bright young man, was accepted at age 11 to Harvard in 1909, as part of an experimental program for extremely young boys who showed exceptional aptitude. He had a reputation as a mathematical genius who had mastered algebra, trigonometry, geometry, and calculus by age ten; however, Sidis also had a naturally fragile emotional state and an overbearing father who pushed him for fame and celebrity, sometimes even making wild claims to visiting reporters such as claiming that his son could speak roughly 40 different languages (which was later found to be false). The newly emergent national media latched on to Sidis as a budding celebrity, chronicling his accomplishments at Harvard as a human-interest story with a positive spin, at first. In time though, young William began to struggle with fame and his documented emotional problems began to emerge, manifesting as bouts of depression and extreme anxiety. Graduating at the age of 16, his life became increasingly turbulent after that point. He was asked to leave graduate school at Rice University after three years of terrible teaching reviews, dropped out of law school, was arrested for participating in a socialist May Day parade that turned violent, was committed to a sanatorium for mental health reasons, and died at the age of 46, after spending most of his life surviving off the pittance he could earn from doing menial tasks and minor mechanical repair work. The media, which could be so fickle even then, went from treating him as a darling in the early years to holding him up as a figure of ridicule, running occasional nationally syndicated pieces concerning Sidis' increasing eccentricities, failures, and struggles. He became a household name of sorts, with the term "Sidis" even becoming a common slang term used to describe someone who failed to live up to expectations. Unfortunately, the media portrayed his failures as an example of the effects of academic acceleration upon children without the consideration of such variables as the effects of parenting practices, emotional disorders, and irresponsible media practices. Regardless, within two decades of Sidis' emotional collapse, early entrance to college had become rare and was viewed by most as a dangerous practice, rife with social and emotional pitfalls that could irrevocably damage a child's well-being. On a side note, it is interesting to mention that the media spent little time talking about any of the other, more successful young men who were admitted to Harvard at exceptionally young ages as part of that institution's "experiment" or discussing how those early educational challenges may have helped their talents to flourish. After all, surely the lives of Sidis' classmates Buckminster Fuller (architect, inventor, author, futurist, and president of MENSA) and Roger Sessions (musicologist, composer, critic, and Pulitzer Prize winner) might provide an alternate view.

Early entrance had gone from being widespread and accepted as the norm in the 1800s to being seen as unusual and suspicious by the 1930s. The 1940s saw a major reversal of opinion once again, this time due to the increased economic and military needs caused by America's entrance into World War II. As the Selective Training and Service Act of 1940 began to put pressure on American businesses that were losing skilled employees to the military draft, the business sector started to pressure educational institutions in turn, in the hopes that they would find quicker ways of educating young men, and thereby, provide speedy replacements for the dwindling workforce.[5] Additionally, the military also pressured educators for speed and found ways to encourage early entrance, although their motives stemmed from desiring new officer candidates to replace those killed in the fighting. By the time of America's entrance into the war in 1941, three universities had already established early-entrance programs and many more followed their lead after the attack on Pearl Harbor.[6]

While the pressures of wartime had helped to restore the practice of early college entrance and resulted in the formation of several short-lived "early entrance programs," the fabric once again began to unravel following the war's conclusion. In the years after peace was restored, public sentiment quickly turned against early entrance, this time due to the (successful) effects of the "G.I. Bill," which provided low-interest loans to returning veterans for use in establishing businesses or attending college. A flood of servicemen entered the university system through the latter half of the 1940s, and many parents and educators were uncomfortable with the notion of atypically young early entrants sharing classrooms and dormitories with experienced veterans in their twenties and thirties. As such, early entrance programs dissipated until the early 1950s, when renewed military conflict in Korea once again created an economic and military need for rapid education and workplace training.

Central to the efforts of the 1950s were the academic preparedness and scholarship programs of the Ford Foundation, whose initiatives resulted in three major changes for early entrance.[7] First, in the hopes of encouraging bright students to enter college early, the Ford Foundation began to offer scholarships to students who met college admissions criteria yet were younger than 16.5 years of age. Second, to support the students and provide incentives for colleges to accept these young applicants, the Foundation funded the establishment of 12 early entrance programs at colleges across the nation. Third, to improve the college readiness of students who were not yet prepared to fully matriculate to higher education, the foundation also established and funded the College Board Advanced Placement (AP) Program, thus bringing college-level courses to regular high schools through the Advanced Placement Program.[8] Following the eventual de-escalation of the Korean conflict the Ford Foundation ceased funding these initiatives, and early entrance once again became less common. Interestingly enough, however, all 12 of the partner colleges who had received Ford Foundation grants have since continued to accept early applicants, even without continuing their official programs.

While early entrance ebbed in overall popularity and frequency during the 1960s and 1970s, the nation's first modern early entrance programs were actually established during this time. In contrast to the temporary programs that had been supported by the Ford Foundation, which were mainly used as recruiting tools and left students to their own devices upon arrival, these new commuter and residential programs were specifically entrusted with the task of providing ongoing services and support for their young charges' academic, social, and emotional well-being. The first of these institutions was Simon's Rock College, which was founded in 1966 to cater entirely to young gifted students. The University of Washington then followed suit in 1977, founding their "Early Entrance Program" (EEP) for students age 12-14, and in 1978 Clarkson University invited 17 year olds to skip their final year of high school in favor of the Clarkson University "Bridging Year Program." Each program developed a reputation as a success, remains in operation today, and other institutions were quick to join the trend. The next three decades would see tremendous growth for this early entrance programming model, and from 1980 to 2013 the number of residential and commuter programs nationwide rose from 3 to at least 19, depending on how one defines the term "early entrance program." More so, surveys by Fluitt and Strickland[9] have shown that approximately 87% of American colleges and universities reported periodically admitting young, qualified applicants who did not possess a high school diploma even in the absence of an official program.

Early entrance to college, historically, always has been subject to many of the same patterns of acceptance and rejection that characterized gifted education in general in the United States. During times of peace, calm, and stability, the national mood tends to turn towards the promotion of equity-based concerns with a focus on the worthy goal of promoting quality learning opportunities for students at all levels, but especially for those who may be struggling or may be in need of greater support. During times of war, stress, or uncertainty, the national mood swings in favor of educational programs that promote excellence, in terms of helping to better foster the talents of our nation's brightest or most promising students. What has been quite remarkable is that the "new wave" of residential and commuter-based programs, which have rapidly multiplied since 1983, seem to be bucking this trend. In contrast to the experimental programs that young men like William James Sidis attended, these modern programs provide extensive support and guidance for their participants. In contrast to the military-university partnerships of the 1940s that were designed with a singular, officer-commissioning purpose in mind, modern programs seek to educate students according to their specific interests and future goals, whatever those may be, by connecting them to the type of challenging, full curriculum that would be otherwise unavailable on their high school campus. And in contrast to the temporary early entrance programs of the 1950s funded by the Ford Foundation, these modern programs are here for the long haul, quickly and quietly becoming a permanent fixture in the American collegiate landscape. In other words, their history has been rocky, but their future looks bright.[10]

EARLY ENTRANCE TO COLLEGE: MYTH VS. FACT

Since the early twentieth century the concept of radical acceleration has been accompanied by many negative connotations, bringing to mind the image of pushy parents "robbing" their offspring of their childhoods and demanding more than nature intended. In recent decades these negative perceptions have been fueled by books such as *The Hurried Child: Growing Up too Fast too Soon* by Dr. David Elkind and tabloid reporting about child stars who crumpled under the weight of success and fell prey to drugs, alcohol, and other temptations. As a result of these popular perceptions, the vast majority of American parents and teachers say that they are opposed to grade skipping fearing for students' social and emotional well-being even though they have not had personal experience with the issue. Common thought, it seems, leads most to suspect that students of a particular chronological age naturally belong with students of that same chronological age, and that separation from age peers exposes them to considerable personal risks.

The trepidation of parents and teachers alike, when it comes to recommending grade skipping or early college entrance, should certainly be understood as well-intentioned. Adults want children in their care to fit in and enjoy their youth, growing to be well-adjusted among same-age peers. What they likely do not realize, however, is that this goal may not be achieved for some gifted students in traditional age/grade assignments. While classroom popularity is somewhat correlated with having slightly higher than average intelligence, and the vast majority of gifted students fall within an IQ range that Hollingworth[11] once called the zone of "socially optimal intelligence" (125 to 155), some students with exceptionally high IQs face the potential of social rejection by their same age peers. While highly precocious, extremely bright learners are typically accepted by other students during elementary school, their stark cognitive differences may begin to exact a price as the students reach middle school age. These students are not unaware of their social standing, and many begin to internalize the difference and blame themselves for their relational difficulties. By the time that these exceptionally talented students reach high school they will often do anything to escape the dreaded "nerd" label, even if that means masking their abilities through humor or rebellion, intentionally underachieving academically, or abandoning prior interests in extracurricular activities to avoid rejection.[12]

Little do these gifted students realize that their struggles to find meaningful relationships with classmates mirror the adult realization that physical age similarity is not the tie that binds. That is, some gifted adolescents find the most satisfying social life evolves with students who are chronologically older than they are. These positive social interactions are often a result of shared interests. For example, consider the case of seventeen year-old Jada, a shy young woman and successful early entrant in her second year of college. Jada shared with me that as a poor-yet-brilliant African American girl growing up in a struggling school system, she had been lonely from kindergarten until she left school. Why, she would ask, was she the only third grader with an interest in Shakespeare? Why weren't the other children awkwardly hiding Macbeth under their desks, as she was, instead of listening to the teacher say the same thing again and again at the blackboard?   It wasn't until leaving high school early and enrolling in college that Jada was able to forge significant friendships, both with similarly advanced teens and older university students who shared her interests and goals.

We will examine further the social case for early college entrance later in this section, but it is critical to mention that many common objections that parents and teachers have to radical acceleration are based in academic concerns as well.[13] Routine academic arguments against grade skipping often include worries that children will find the new curriculum too demanding or fast-paced, that knowledge gaps in their understandings of a topic will render them unable to successfully learn or achieve, that students will miss out on aspects of the "invisible curriculum" and wisdom shared by their regular teachers, or that students' giftedness may somehow fade over time, leaving them unprepared and at a great disadvantage in later study. Additionally practical concerns are commonly raised as well, ranging from fears that students will need to make serious career decisions at an earlier age, may have difficulty getting hired for prestigious jobs or being taken seriously at work if they look too young, may not be ready in terms of their personal emotional and maturity-based characteristics for independent living, or may even look back and regret missing key societal milestones such as going to the prom or playing a varsity sport.

While some of these concerns likely have merit, such as worries that students may not be ready to make major career decisions or may have additional difficulty competing for high-level jobs if they graduate from college at 18 or 19 rather than 21 or 22, several others have been refuted.[14] Consider, for example, that most early entrants earn, on average, a higher college GPA than the traditionally aged students who surround them in their classes. Findings such as these generally discount the notions that knowledge gaps or increased curricular demands complicate the path to success for most early entrants. Additionally, concerns that early entrants will find themselves drowning in material too intellectually advanced are often denied by actual early entrants, who are far more likely to state that they had been waiting their whole lives for rigorous, engaging content, and that college had finally provided to them what elementary school, middle school, and high school had not. To continue with our turn from supposition and conjecture, let us now examine the findings in the research on acceleration, including early entrance to college, relating to students' academic and social experiences.

Academically, the past four decades have seen the publication of more than 300 research studies that have collectively demonstrated that acceleration measures such as grade skipping and early college entrance can be an extremely positive choice for ability-appropriate intellectual development in gifted students.[15] Accelerated students have been found on average to progress farther and faster through schooling, to earn higher GPA's in college, to carrier heavier credit loads, to earn honors such as making the Dean's List at a greater rate, and to graduate more quickly than the general college population. Additionally, early entrance accelerants have been found to hold higher post-graduate aspirations including more frequently expressed intents to attend graduate or professional schools than their traditionally aged classmates, to apply to these schools at a higher rate, to earn acceptance at a higher rate, and to successfully graduate from these institutions at a higher rate. Early entrants have also been found to commonly report a sense of euphoria upon having acclimated to the more intellectual atmosphere of university life, having finally found a place where they could stretch their abilities to the limit and interact with intellectual peers for perhaps the very first time. The reasons for their joy seem well supported by the research literature as a whole, as made evident by two well-known meta-analyses by Kulik and Kulik, The first of these research projects[16] compared 26 published studies on the academic performance of accelerated students and found that in every study the accelerants had academically outperformed their non-accelerated peers. The second project[17] compared the effects of acceleration with the demonstrated benefits of another popular method of servicing advanced learners, known as enrichment. Kulik and Kulik concluded that acceleration's benefits had twice as powerful an impact upon the students' later academic performance. In fact, one of the researchers would later state that the academic effects of acceleration upon gifted learners' performance were among the strongest statistical results he had ever seen in published literature.

Socially, in contrast to the fears of most teachers and parents that early entrants would have great difficulty fitting in and relating to their older classmates, research has typically found that acceleration is usually surprisingly neutral in its effects.[18] Investigations into the experiences of independently matriculated early entrants have generally shown that they have experienced on average no more social or emotional difficulties than typical students of their age and intellectual ability. More so, they have been found to be generally well-suited to college life, exhibiting no additional adaptation difficulties on average than those of typical, traditionally aged freshmen. In fact, due to the varying degrees of physical development that can be found across adolescents in general, many older early entrants are surprised to find that older students simply assume that the accelerated "look young" rather than assuming that they skipped their last year or two of high school. While studies of acceleration have not typically shown net gains in accelerants' socialization abilities, self-esteem has been shown to be enhanced during short-term situations such as acceleration-based summer camps, and in longer-term acceleration settings as well.

Prospective early entrants and their parents should be aware that although the majority of studies concerning early entrants' social and emotional adjustments are positive or neutral in nature, a few studies have uncovered specific pitfalls of acceleration. First, early entrants who look especially young or are three-or-more years younger than their classmates may find certain social doors in college closed to them as a function of their age.[19] The opportunities, including fraternity and sorority membership and varsity athletic participation, help to account for the fact that early entrants are slightly less involved in extracurricular activities than college students of a typical age. Second, even when accepted by others for being an especially young student there is a possibility of not being taken seriously or treated with respect, and some early entrants do find themselves being treated as a "floor mascot" or a similar object of curiosity.[20] Third, it is important to note that nearly all issues of social participation and acceptance that early entrance face are actually more likely to hamper males than females, as younger females are more likely to find older boyfriends who can provide access to the general university social network rather than the other way around.[21]

While parents and teachers alike may commonly reject the notions of grade skipping and early college entrance based on gut-feelings and "common sense" worries for students' academic and socio-emotional growth, the research suggests that their well-intentioned fears are largely unfounded. In contrast, acceleration strategies such as early college entrance have been found to be among the most powerful academic strategies available to gifted learners. Further, students seem to either break-even or benefit socially. From this vantage point, it is little wonder that researchers who have asked those most in the know regarding early entrance – the students themselves – find overwhelmingly affirmative responses from those asked, in most cases producing "yes" responses from 80-100% of the respondents.[22] Perhaps it is time to retire William James Sidis as the "poster boy" for acceleration and replace him with a more representative figure such as Dr. Martin Luther King Jr., who entered Morehouse College at the age of 15, without a high school diploma, after skipping both the ninth and twelfth grade years. Early entrants, of course, are not guaranteed Dr. King's high levels of success and accomplishment, but they do tend to be successful and accomplished in their own ways, more often than not.

MODERN EARLY ENTRANCE PROGRAMS

While collegiate early entrance for most of our nation's history was primarily an independent undertaking or was accomplished through Ford Foundation type "programs" that provided little support once the students had arrived on campus, the experience of most modern early entrants is sharply different, in a positive way. That difference results from the development of residential early entrance programs at colleges and universities across the United States. These programs provide a wealth of services unavailable to the early entrants of the past including academic tutoring and guidance, social events, emotional counseling to ease the transition, separate residential facilities or classroom space, and in some cases a structured "transition year" that helps early entrants to ease their way into the rigors and challenges of collegiate life. Even more impressively, a great number of modern early entrance programs cater to students of a specific age range, sex, or academic interest, thus helping to ensure that the students are receiving the academic and social support that will most assuredly help them to achieve their dreams. Several, for example, exist solely for the benefit of students interested in focusing in math, science, or engineering. Others admit students who are more interested in the humanities, liberal arts, or leadership. Some cater to the exceptionally young, such as college students between the ages of eleven and fourteen, while most typically admit students between the ages of 15 and 17. A few are open only to students from their own state, while the majority accept applications from students across the nation and globe. As mentioned earlier, the exact number of modern early entrance programs is notoriously difficult to pin down, as a great deal depends on the services one deems essential when determining which colleges provide enough support to be considered as having "programs" rather than a high number of independently matriculated accelerants. Additionally, new early entrance programs have been emerging faster than ever in recent years, making the Internet a good first step when looking for early entrance programs suited to a student's particular needs. Still, the list of programs in Table 1, adapted from prior research by Muratori,[23] should be of use to any student, parent, teacher, or counselor who is interested in learning more about what offerings may be available.

Table 1. Early Entrance Programs

Program Name	Host University	Typical Student Age Ranges
Commuter Programs		
The Early Entrance Program	University of Washington	12-15
UW Academy for Young Scholars	University of Washington	16-17
Early Entrance Program	California State University of Los Angeles	11-17
Boston University Academy	Boston University	13-17
Early College at Guilford	Guilford College	14-17
Bard High School Early College	Bard College	14-17
Early Honors Program	Alaska Pacific University	17-18

Residential Programs		
Advanced Academy of Georgia	University of West Georgia	16-18
Georgia Academy of Math, Engineering, and Science	Middle Georgia College	16-18
Texas Academy of Math and Science	University of North Texas	16-18
Texas Academy of Leadership in the Humanities	Lamar University	16-18
Missouri Academy of Science, Math, and Computing	Northwest Missouri State University	16-18
Clarkson School Bridging Year Program	Clarkson University	17-18
Program for the Exceptionally Gifted	Mary Baldwin College	14-17 (females only)
Simon's Rock College	Bard College	16-20
Resident Honors Program	University of Southern California	17-18
The Gatton Academy of Mathematics and Science	Western Kentucky University	16-18
National Academy of Arts, Sciences, and Engineering	The University of Iowa	17-18
Kansas Academy of Math and Science	Fort Hayes State University	16-18

Admissions Requirements

Admission requirements for early entrance depend largely on where and how a prospective early entrant has chosen to submit an application. For students interested in independent matriculation without a cohort-based program or any special guidance or treatment, there are generally no special application or entrance requirements. Prospective early entrants need only to complete the regular application form, and the vast majority of American colleges and universities are willing to accept them if they can demonstrate that they are at least as well prepared and qualified as the typical freshman applicant. In contrast, students hoping to matriculate to an established early entrance program usually submit a specifically designed application directly to that program and are screened through a separate process that bypasses the university admissions office. Admissions requirements vary from program to program and incorporate a wide range of assessments. The process usually begins by asking whether the student's age corresponds to the educational mission of the program. Programs vary with regard to the age range of students they are willing to accept, and while some such as the University of Washington's Early Entrance Program and Mary Baldwin College's Program for the Exceptionally Gifted are designed to cater to the especially young, most early entrance programs only rarely accept students below the age of 15 or 16 unless the evidence clearly indicates that the student's maturity level and interpersonal skills will make that student a good fit on campus.

The admission process at most early entrance programs incorporates several elements, including SAT/ACT scores, grades from high and/or middles school that reflect courses taken and high school grade point average (if high school was attended), class rank if applicable, personal statements, letters of recommendation, and usually an interview or series of interviews – often combined with a mandatory visit to campus. The use of standardized tests, grades, essays, and recommendations is traditional to college admissions overall, and applicants are generally held to admissions standards at least as high as those applied to the university's general admissions pool, if not the standards of the university's honors program or college. The one element that differs significantly for most early entrance program applicants is the requirement of a school visit and interview. Additionally, many programs opt to interview both the student and his or her parents. The interviews are considered to be a critical component of the admissions process by most early entrance programs and are undertaken in the hopes of yielding information regarding the student's maturity level and social and emotional preparedness for collegiate life. Additionally, visits and interviews with both the applicant and parents often highlight whether the student or the parents are actually the driving force behind the application, and whether the student is interested in making this move for mature, responsible reasons.

One final consideration worth mentioning within the admissions context is the fact that early entrance to some colleges and universities is limited by the geographic home of the student. Certain programs have been established and maintained through state or municipal educational funding, for example, and only accept students who are residents of that state or city as a result. The Texas Academy of Math and Science, the Bard High School Early College program of New York City, and the Gatton Academy of Mathematics and Science in Kentucky are examples. Additionally, while it is common at many early entrance programs for as many as half of the students to eventually transfer to other universities to complete their degree, some programs have taken steps to prevent this from occurring. One reason why universities are willing to host early entrance programs in the first place is because they want to attract exceptionally bright students, and schools such as the University of Iowa make clear to applicants that their acceptance is predicated on a goodwill assumption that they will not seek to transfer to another institution.

Support Structures

In considering application and eventual early matriculation, the next major question for students and their families to consider is the types of facilities and support structures that are available. Early entrance programs vary significantly in the degrees of academic, social, and emotional support that they provide for their students, but most tend to follow a theory of "optimal match," as researchers Noble and Childers[24] labeled it, meaning that they seek to create a nurturing, supportive environment that meets the needs of their specific population of students on all three of those developmental continua.

While not every early entrance program is residential, at least ten colleges in the United States maintain a separate dormitory to house young men and young women who are younger than the general college population. The size and utility of these facilities differs greatly depending by institution, but most include standard living spaces, student lounges, and facilities to be used for program events and activities. These dormitories usually enforce a higher level of social rules and expectations than found in general university housing, such as maintaining curfew hours, separating the sexes, and employing a specialized team of residential assistants who are hired and trained specifically to work with younger students.

Program administrators and students alike often take great pride in their residential facilities, as well as in the sense of cohesion and identity that it breeds among program participants and alumni. Fostering this sense of belonging can be crucial to helping students feel connected to their new educational surroundings, and as a result, several programs struggle with the question of whether or not to allow students to return home on the weekends. Some programs allow students to come and go as they please, while others only allow a maximum of one visit home per month.

Apart from residential facilities, perhaps the most important support factor commonly offered by early entrance programs is that of specialized guidance and counseling to support the social and emotional development of younger college students. Providing such support is a major departure from the historical practice of treating early entrants strictly as typical freshmen. Modern programs, in contrast, recognize that their population's unique situation presents them with unique challenges as well, and social and emotional counseling opportunities thus become an important piece of the overall picture. In addition to training the university's general mental health and counseling professionals on the differences of early entrance students, these programs typically employ at least one in-house counselor as well. Some programs even employ two such individuals full time, one to provide academic counseling and the other for socio-emotional interventions. This arrangement is seen as a valuable tool in supporting students' development, as regular involvement between the counselors and students ideally creates a more comfortable atmosphere, making it easier for students to approach the counselors for guidance and/or conversation.

In addition to counseling opportunities, another support structure that is often found at early entrance programs for the exceptionally young (13-15) is that of a "transitional year," which blends the college and high school environment and shelters students from full collegiate immersion until they have become comfortable with their new surroundings over the course of nine months. Newcomers to the University of Washington and Mary Baldwin College, for example, spend one year with a mix of college and high school level coursework before enrolling in college full-time, during which time they receive specialized counseling services as well.

In addition to residential facilities, specialized residential staff, counseling opportunities, and transitional programs, a number of other support factors also can be found at many early entrance programs:[25]

- A select group of early entrance programs have negotiated the possibility for students to align their college schedules with state high school graduation requirements, thus allowing program participants to take a full slate of college-level coursework while receiving both college credit and an eventual high school diploma. Some state-run early entrance programs have even been given the authority to confer their own high school diplomas in addition to associate's degrees.

- Early entrance programs nationwide regularly offer social, cultural, and recreational trips and experiences such as dances, movie marathons, game watches, holiday festivities, and bus trips to plays and museums.

- Early entrance students at most colleges are given nearly full access to the social, cultural, and athletic life of college, with the only two exceptions being a ban on joining fraternities or sororities and the inability to play NCAA sanctioned, intercollegiate sports due to restrictions imposed by the NCAA. Apart from those exceptions, students' personal lives and interests are supported through participation in normal collegiate clubs, organizations, and intramural sports competitions.

- Several residential programs automatically enroll their students in the host campus's honors college, thereby providing increased academic support even after the student has entered the general student body and left the early entrance dorm behind.

- While early entrance programs typically carry an annual tuition ranging from $3,105 to more than $30,000, almost every residential program makes available a number of need-based scholarships in addition to any merit-based awards they may possess. Interestingly, early entrance programs sometimes argue that the high cost of attending these programs may be more than offset by the additional year(s) of income that a graduate earns over the course of their extended career.

IS EARLY ENTRANCE THE RIGHT FIT?

When students who have entered college early go home for breaks and see their old classmates around town, a common question they are asked is "Why?" Some of us might ask why a high school student would elect to turn away from all the trappings of that special age, such as Friday night football games, the school play, the prom, and graduation parties, and leave early for something more challenging. When people ask that question, however, they are forgetting some simple truths in life: That what is enjoyable for one person may not be enjoyable for another, that what might be intellectually stimulating to one student might be mind-numbingly boring to another, and that what might provide thrilling social opportunities to one child might offer isolated, lonely nights to another. In short, early entrants often choose to pursue college at a young age because they are in an environment that does not quite fit, and they wish to find an environment that does. For some early entrants, boredom and dissatisfaction with the standard (or even advanced) high school curriculum underscored the academic differences between themselves and their age-mates.[26] For others, it was the difficulty they experienced in forming mutually meaningful social relationships with others of their own chronological age.[27] That is not to say that all early entrants did not have good teachers or fine friends – many of them certainly did have one, if not both, of those things. But having peers with whom you can talk about sports and television does not necessarily challenge a person intellectually in the way that others with similar intellectual interests might. Extremely bright students often know that there are opportunities for them to learn with others who think in the same ways and care about the same things, where classes are not only challenging but engaging as well – and they thirst for that experience. This is especially true when talented students previously attended a residential summer program for the gifted where they were able to take classes on a college campus with other advanced students and found how fulfilling that experience could be, if only for a brief period of time.

In addition to these two common motivators for entering college early, i.e. dissatisfaction with the standard curriculum and a lack of social compatibility, there is often a third reason, especially among early entrants who go on to be successful in their new collegiate environment. This third motivator is the recognition that making the leap to college will help them in a practical sense to achieve their academic goals more quickly, whatever those may be.[28] A high percentage of early entrants hope to attend graduate or professional school, and many realize that early entrance will trim one, two, or perhaps more years off of the total amount of time they will ultimately need to be in school, while making their résumé more attractive. Others may simply want extra time to spend in college, out of a desire to study many different disciplines. One young man I interviewed had matriculated to college at the age of 14 and was in his third year of university work. He explained to me that he was glad to have entered college early because he wanted to become a physicist at the CERN Laboratory in Switzerland. To be successful in his pursuit of that goal, he had decided to quadruple major in math, physics, French, and German. "It will take me five years to do that," he explained, "but I figure that's ok."

PREDICTING SUCCESS OF EARLY COLLEGE ENTRANTS

Aside from the practical advantages to early entrance, there are other factors that may help to predict success as an early entrant. While there are plenty of gifted young men and women who might feel ready for college, it is unlikely that all of those students would be successful at handling the intellectual rigors of a full-time college course load or would feel comfortable attempting friendships with students two or three years their senior. While there is no set formula for determining which students would thrive as an early entrant, both research studies and anecdotal evidence suggest that four factors may make a meaningful difference"

1. Does the student desire to enter college early?

While this critical factor may seem like a given, this is unfortunately not the case. From time to time, parents may push their child to take this step against the child's wishes, in the hopes that early matriculation would provide their son or daughter with a better education, a better social environment, or a better résumé. While early entrance to college can provide students with those benefits, it is highly unlikely to do so if the child does not actually want to participate. This is because college matriculation, when it comes down to it, is very much an independent affair. Parents may push their child to enter college early, but after the student has moved into the dormitory and farewells have been exchanged, students of any age will need personal drive and intrinsic motivation in order to achieve at the collegiate level. In other words, unwilling or unenthusiastic students may enter college early, but they are unlikely to enjoy the experience, to thrive, or even to persevere for the long term. Recognition of this fact has led most modern early entrance programs to adopt the habit of requiring campus visits that include interviews with both a potential applicant and his or her parents. While the vast majority of applicants are the driving force behind their own application, interview committees do occasionally find that the moment an applicant's parents leave the room the student quietly asks them to deny their application. In many cases this occurs when the student who has applied feels a "good fit" with his or her current educational environment and feels reluctant to leave behind classes he or she is enjoying, an extracurricular activity that would be missed, or even a network of good friends who are supportive.

2. Is the student sufficiently emotionally mature?

Both parents and teachers of the gifted know that it is surprisingly easy to assume that students of advanced intellectual abilities must or should be more advanced than their peers in an emotional sense as well, yet this is often not the case. A fifteen-year-old student with a perfect SAT score is still fifteen years old. At times, he or she will do and say things that from an adult perspective are completely unacceptable, yet from a fifteen-year-old are to be expected. While it would be unrealistic to hold any atypically young early entrant to the emotional maturity standards that we would expect of an older student, there is undoubtedly a natural range of maturity within the younger group as well. Some young men and women seem to have greater emotional control regardless of their age, others may need more time to grow and develop. Early entrants who have more advanced senses of personal emotional maturity, in terms of understanding themselves, their goals, the need for behavioral boundaries and restraint, and the importance of delayed gratification to academic accomplishment (working hard now for potential rewards later) tend to be in a better position for success.

3. *Is the student comfortable with early independence?*

Leaving home and living on your own for the first time is a scary endeavor, regardless of one's age. It is normal and natural to expect jittery feelings as the big day approaches and even to experience the pain of homesickness for the first few weeks or even a month or two. Students who have had prior life experiences apart from their families and friends often acclimate more easily to their new surroundings, while students whose experiences have been more insular or dependent on others may have a greater difficulty in finding comfort in living on their own. For these reasons, some of the most successful early entrants I have dealt with have been students from military households whose families moved regularly across the U.S. or even the world. Periodic social uprooting became part of these students' lives, and leaving home to move into a college dorm just seemed like another such transition.

4. *What is the student's level of academic preparedness prior to entering college life?*

While all early entrants tend to share the experience of boredom with their standard high school curriculum, not all high schools offer the same degree of intellectual rigor or practice when it comes to developing proper study skills. While some students do come to early entrance programs from school settings where the level of academic difficulty was high and students truly did have cause for developing good study habits, a majority of those I have interviewed did not and therefore had to adapt. Students who quickly recognize this need and work to improve their study skills are typically successful. Those who fall prey to habits of procrastination, skipping classes, and cramming for tests, however, often learn the hard way that college requires increased time, effort, and responsibility than they may have been able to get by on in the past.

While the factors discussed above seem to contribute meaningfully to an early entrant's chances for success, it is important to note that early entrance programs are well aware of these facts and have sharply honed applicant screening procedures in order increase the likelihood of accepting students with the greatest chance of success. As a result, the attrition rates at major early entrance facilities have dramatically declined over the past 30 years, in some cases going from as high as 50 percent down to less than 5 percent. One of the most significant reasons for this incredible improvement has been that new programs have tended to better clarify their own sense of institutional identity, clearly defining what type of program they seek to be and therefore what type of student they hope to attract, accept, and serve. In other words, as stated earlier, the programs have adopted a philosophy that researchers often label as optimal match. When evaluating each applicant, they ask not whether the applicant has the brainpower to earn straight A's, but rather whether the applicant's intellect, academic goals, personality, emotional maturity, commitment, study skills, and comfort with early independence would likely lead them to be successful within the context of that particular program.

Parents, teachers, and guidance counselors who hope to aid bright young men or women in their quest to enter college early would do well to adopt this philosophy of optimal match to aid the prospective applicants in finding an environment that provides a good fit. Colleges and universities all across the country differ from each other in many key respects, as do the early entrance programs that they house. As potential applicants begin the process of looking for opportunities to enter college early, those mentors would do well to encourage the students to consider a variety of key questions, such as the following:

- Does the student most desire to matriculate independently to a college or university, being treated like any other freshmen, or are they looking for a program with greater structural support in terms of both academics and social events?

- If the student would prefer a structured program, is she or he willing to accept the extra behavioral rules, such as having a curfew and not being able to visit friends of the opposite sex after a certain hour, which often go along with that decision?

- If the student is hoping for a structured program, would he/she prefer a commuter program or a residential program?

- Does the student wish to remain close to home or is the student willing to move far from home if necessary?

- Does the student have a particular interest or career goal that fits an early entrance program that specializes in math and science, or would the student be more interested in programs that encourage study of the liberal arts or humanities?

- Are there particular majors, programs, or extracurricular activities that the student cares about deeply and wants to pursue? If so, care must be taken to ensure that those opportunities are available on each particular campus.

- Does the student wish to stay at the hosting university after completing the early entrance program, which typically encompasses the first two years of study, or does the student hope to transfer to another university afterwards? Different programs have different policies regarding transfers.

- Is the student prepared to apply to and visit multiple campuses, in order to identify the university or program that offers the best fit?

CONCLUSION

More than four decades of educational research has shown early entrance to college to be one of the most powerfully positive educational opportunities available to gifted learners. While many parents, teachers, and counselors still oppose radical acceleration techniques such as grade skipping and early college entrance based on fears that students will be unable to keep up with the advanced academic material and/or succeed socially among older students, research has demonstrated that neither of these common concerns has merit. Academically, early college entrants outperform their non-accelerated classmates in virtually every measure. They take more classes, earn higher grades, graduate more quickly, hold higher career aspirations, are accepted by graduate and professional schools at a higher rate, and graduate from those post-baccalaureate programs at a higher rate as well. Meanwhile, research into accelerants' social lives has continually discovered a roughly neutral effect, meaning that while students' do not experience rapid improvement they do not seem to be negatively affected by early entrance either. More so, there is anecdotal evidence to suggest that social improvement may be increasingly common as time goes on, due to the fact that much of the research on students' social experiences was conducted prior to, or early into, the rise of the modern early entrance program.

Rather than having early entrants matriculate as regular freshmen with little to no extra support, modern programs provide a mix of specialized dormitories, disciplinary guidance with a trained residential staff, special class facilities, social events, academic counseling, social and emotional counseling, shared meals, extracurricular activities, and a variety of other services and supportive bonding experiences. Students who enter college early through programs such as these often report a sense of joy at finally finding both classes that challenge them academically and friends who share their common interests and passions.

Students who choose to matriculate to college at an atypically young age, whether independently or in a structured program, typically do so because of boredom and dissatisfaction with their traditional high school curriculum and/or difficulty in making quality social connections with same-age peers. Those who are most successful often matriculate for practical reasons as well, typically regarding a desire to begin studying a topic of interest or using early entrance as a stepping stone to a rewarding career, graduate or professional school, or an eventual transfer to another undergraduate institution. Additionally, students who are most successful as early applicants tend to strongly desire the experience, to be emotionally mature for their age, to be comfortable with the experience of living independently, and to be well prepared for college in terms of both academic content knowledge and study skills. Students, parents, teachers, and counselors are invited to reexamine their previous beliefs concerning early entrance, considering why Dr. James Borland, fully aware of the pervasive fears regarding grade skipping and early college entrance, wrote the following after examining the research concerning the topic:

"Acceleration is one of the most curious phenomena in the field of education. I can think of no other issue in which there is such a gulf between what research has revealed and what most practitioners believe. The research on acceleration is so uniformly positive, the benefits of appropriate acceleration so unequivocal, that it is difficult to see how an educator could oppose it."[29]

ENDNOTES

[1] Robinson, K. (2008). *Changing paradigms* [video file]. Retrieved from http://www.thersa.org/events/video/archive/sir-ken-robinson

[2] Kett, J. (1974). History of age grouping in America. In J. S. Coleman (Ed.), *Youth: Transition to adulthood. A report of the Panel on Youth of the President's Science Advisory Committee* (pp. 6-29; Publication No. 4106-00037). Washington, DC: U.S. Government Printing Office.

[3] Oden, M. H. (1968). The fulfillment of promise: 40-year follow-up of the Terman gifted group. *Genetic Psychology Monographs, 77*, 3-93.

[4] Southern, W. T., & Jones, E. D. (1991). *The academic acceleration of gifted children*. New York, NY: Teachers College Press.

[5] Southern, W. T., & Jones, E. D. (1991). *The academic acceleration of gifted children*. New York, NY: Teachers College Press.

[6] Colangelo, N., Assouline, S., Gross, M. U. M. (2004). *A nation deceived: How schools hold back America's brightest students*. Iowa City, IA: The Connie Belin & Jacqueline N. Blank International Center for Gifted Education and Talent Development.

[7] Southern, W. T., & Jones, E. D. (1991). *The academic acceleration of gifted children*. New York, NY: Teachers College Press.

[8] Muratori, M. C. (2007). *Early entrance to college: A guide to success*. Waco, TX: Prufrock Press.

[9] Fluitt, J. L., & Strickland, M. S. (1984). A survey of early admission policies and procedures. *College and University, 59*, 129-135.

[10] For more information regarding the history of early entrance programs, see: Colangelo, N., Assouline, S., Gross, M. U. M. (2004). *A nation deceived: How schools hold back America's brightest students*. Iowa City, IA: The Connie Belin & Jacqueline N. Blank International Center for Gifted Education and Talent Development, and Muratori, M. (2007). *Early entrance to college: A guide to success*. Waco, TX: Prufrock Press.

[11] Hollingworth, L. S. (1942). *Children above IQ 180: Their origin and development*. New York, NY: World Books.

[12] Davis, G. A., & Rimm, S. B. (1998). *Education of the gifted and talented*. Needham Heights, MA: Allyn & Bacon.

[13] Additional discussion concerning common objections to early entrance may be found in Southern, W. T., & Jones, E. D. (1991). *The academic acceleration of gifted children*. New York, NY: Teachers College Press, and Muratori, M. C. (2007). Early entrance to college: A guide to success. Waco, TX: Prufrock Press.

[14] See the following for greater discussion on the demonstrated benefits of early college entrance: Gross, M. U. M., & van Vliet, H. E. (2005). Radical acceleration and early entrance to college: A review of the research. *Gifted Child Quarterly, 49*, 154-171, and Olszewski-Kubilius, P. (2002). A summary of research regarding early entrance to college. *Roeper Review, 24*(3), 152-157.

[15] Colangelo, N., Assouline, S., Gross, M. U. M. (2004). *A nation deceived: How schools hold back America's brightest students*. Iowa City, IA: The Connie Belin & Jacqueline N. Blank International Center for Gifted Education and Talent Development

[16] Kulik, J. A., & Kulik, C. C. (1984). Effects of accelerated instruction on students. *Review of Educational Research, 54*, 409-425.

[17] Kulik, J. A., & Kulik, C. C. (1992). Meta-analytic findings on grouping programs. *Gifted Child Quarterly, 36*, 73-77.

[18] See the following for greater discussion on the social and emotional effects of early college entrance: Gross, M. U. M., & van Vliet, H. E. (2005). Radical acceleration and early entrance to college: A review of the research. *Gifted Child Quarterly, 49*, 154-171, and Olszewski-Kubilius, P. (2002). A summary of research regarding early entrance to college. *Roeper Review, 24*(3), 152-157.

[19] Noble, K. D., Vaughan, R. C., Chan, C., Childers, S., Chow, B., Federow, A., & Hughes, S. (2007). Love and work: The legacy of early university entrance. *Gifted Child Quarterly, 51*, 152-166.

[20] Sayler, M. F. (1992). *Early college entrance for gifted high school students: Experiences and guidelines*. Retrieved from the ERIC database. (ED345395).

[21] Janos, P. M., Robinson, N. M., Carter, C., Chapel, A., Cufley, R., Curland, M., Daily, M., ... & Wise, A. (1998). A cross-sectional

developmental study of the social relations of students who enter college early. *Gifted Child Quarterly, 32,* 210-216.

[22] For more on this, see Gross, M. U. M. (2004). *Exceptionally gifted children* (2nd ed.). London, England: Routledge, and Rimm, S. B., & Lovance, K. J. (1992). The use of subject and grade skipping for the prevention and reversal of underachievement. *Gifted Child Quarterly, 36,* 100-105.

[23] Muratori, M. C. (2007). *Early entrance to college: A guide to success.* Waco, TX: Prufrock Press.

[24] Noble, K. D., & Childers, S. A. (2008). A passion for learning: The theory and practice of optimal match at the University of Washington. *Journal of Advanced Academics, 19,* 236-270.

[25] Additional information regarding institutional support factors at early entrance programs is discussed in Booth, D., Sethna, B. N., Stanley, J. C., & Colgate, S. O. (1999). Special opportunities for exceptionally able high school students: A description of eight residential early-college-entrance programs. *Journal of Secondary Gifted Education, 10*(4), 195-203, and Muratori, M. C. (2007). *Early entrance to college: A guide to success.* Waco, TX: Prufrock Press.

[26] Noble, K. D., & Childers, S. A. (2008). A passion for learning: The theory and practice of optimal match at the University of Washington. *Journal of Advanced Academics, 19,* 236-270.

[27] Noble, K. D., & Drumond, J. E. (1992). But what about the prom? Students' perceptions of early college entrance. *Gifted Child Quarterly, 36,* 106-111.

[28] For more on early entrants' post-college aspirations and accomplishments, see Gross, M. U. M., & van Vliet, H. E. (2005). Radical acceleration and early entrance to college: A review of the research. *Gifted Child Quarterly, 49,* 154-171, and Noble, K. D., Robinson, N. M., & Gunderson, S. A. (1993). All rivers lead to the sea: A follow-up study of gifted young adults. *Roeper Review, 15*(3), 124-130.

[29] Borland, J. H. (1989). *Planning and implementing programs for the gifted* (p. 185). New York, NY: Teachers College Press.

RECOMMENDED RESOURCES

Colangelo, N., Assouline, S. G., Gross, M. U. M. (2004). *A nation deceived: How schools hold back America's brightest students.* Iowa City: University of Iowa, Connie Belin & Jacqueline N. Blank International Center for Gifted Education and Talent Development.

A two-volume report on the benefits of, and need for, the increased use of academic acceleration techniques in American education. The first volume presents the report's arguments and evidence in a reader-friendly manner, aimed at parents and teachers of the gifted. The second volume presents the foundational data behind the report in a scholarly, academic manner more suited for educational researchers.

Gross, M. U. M., & van Vliet, H. E. (2005). Radical acceleration and early entrance to college: A review of the research. *Gifted Child Quarterly, 49,* 154-171.

This review of the literature is especially notable for three important contributions: It presents valuable information concerning radical acceleration practices internationally; it draws conclusions regarding the benefits and pitfalls of radical acceleration from both individual case studies and cohort studies, providing a comprehensive view; and the authors summarize and explain a number of factors that have been found to improve the chances of a successful academic and socio-emotional transition.

Muratori, M. C. (2007). *Early entrance to college: A guide to success.* Waco, TX: Prufrock Press.

This student-friendly text provides adolescents and their parents with information concerning early college entrance opportunities. Questions regarding personal readiness, how to select a program, how to best prepare for the transition, and how to maximize the odds of college life success are all considered and discussed.

Noble, K. D., Childers, S. A., & Vaughan, R. C. (2008). A place to be celebrated and understood: The impact of early university entrance from parents' point of view. *Gifted Child Quarterly, 52,* 256-268.

This research study reports data from a survey of 95 parents of teens enrolled in early entrance programs at the University of Washington. Parents were asked about how they came to see early entrance as a viable option for their students, whether they were satisfied with their children's experiences, what they perceived as the pros and cons of the experience, and how sending a child to college at an early age affected their overall family dynamic.

Olszewski-Kubilius, P. (2002). A summary of research regarding early entrance to college. *Roeper Review, 24,* 152-157.

A review of the literature that examines both early entrants' overall academic performance and their socio-emotional adjustments and general well-being. The article paints a powerful picture of acceleration as a beneficial educational opportunity that brings many benefits to the students involved.

Robinson, K. (2008). *Changing paradigms* [video file].
Retrieved from
http://www.thersa.org/events/video/archive/sir-ken-
robinson

In this hour-long speech, given in response to being
honored with the 2008 Benjamin Franklin Medal by the
Royal Society for the Encouragement of Arts, Manufactures,
and Commerce, Sir Ken Robinson makes the case for moving
beyond our current, outdated educational paradigm based
on theories no longer valid in the modern world. In its place,
Dr. Robinson advocates for adopting a more holistic, group-
oriented educational philosophy that celebrates creativity,
collaboration, and artistic inspiration.

Solow, R., & Rhodes, C. (2012). *College at 13: Young, gifted,
and purposeful.* Scottsdale, AZ: Great Potential Press.

This highly accessible book describes the lives and
experiences of 14 women, all in their 30's, each of whom
had entered college between the ages of 13 and 16. The
women share stories of their experiences as early entrants
and reflect upon how those experiences helped to shape
them into the successful women they eventually became.

ABOUT THE AUTHOR

Alexander Pagnani, Ph.D., is an assistant professor of educational psychology at the University of Central Missouri. He earned his doctorate from the University of Georgia, specializing in gifted education. His dissertation explored life as a collegiate early entrant and involved living in a program's dormitory for four months.

ABOUT THE SERIES EDITOR

Cheryll M. Adams, Ph.D., is the Director Emerita of the Center for Gifted Studies and Talent Development at Ball State University. She has served on the Board of Directors of NAGC and has been president of the Indiana Association for the Gifted and the Association for the Gifted, Council for Exceptional Children.

CPSIA information can be obtained
at www.ICGtesting.com
Printed in the USA
BVHW041851041218
534777BV00009B/565/P